T0196746

100 Things Every Baseball Coach Should Know

BY:

John Stuper

Former World Series Star
And Current College Head Coach

iUniverse, Inc.
New York   Bloomington

100 Things Every Baseball Coach Should Know

iUniverse books may be ordered through booksellers or by contacting:

iUniverse
1663 Liberty Drive
Bloomington, IN 47403
www.iuniverse.com
1-800-Authors (1-800-288-4677)

Because of the dynamic nature of the Internet, any Web addresses or links contained in this book may have changed since publication and may no longer be valid.

ISBN: 978-1-4401-3540-8 (pbk)
ISBN: 978-1-4401-3539-2 (ebk)

Printed in the United States of America

iUniverse rev. date: 4/7/2009

This book is dedicated to my late father, Frank Stuper, who was my first baseball coach. He taught me never to boo, to respect the game, and most importantly, he taught me a love of the game, for which I am eternally grateful.

Contents

Chapter One

Practice

1. Repetitions make a player better.

During your practice time, you should get your players as many "reps" as possible. This includes all positions. In our practices, our infielders probably average taking 200 ground balls a day. You should also have catchers working on blocking, hitters getting extra swings other than batting practice, and outfielders taking a ton of fly balls. These are just a few of the ways to get more repetitions. More will be discussed later, but make no mistake, it is the best way to improve your players on a daily basis.

2. You don't have to hit ground balls from home plate.

In order to get your players a lot of reps, don't get caught in the habit of hitting all of your ground balls from the plate. It can be a waste of time. Go to the pitcher's mound and hit them from there. You will have better control and the shorter distance means more reps. You can even roll them ground balls and that way you have even more control. If you want to work on their backhands or double play feeds or whatever, this is the easiest way to accomplish it. First and third basemen can also benefit from this. Again, getting them reps and making sure they do it correctly is the best way to improve.

3. Work on base running at every practice.

I will devote an entire chapter to base running drills, but let me emphasize right now that base running should be incorporated into every practice. It can mean the difference between a win and a loss in so many games. Many coaches neglect this part of the game.

4. <u>**Don't get caught doing only one thing in practice.**</u>

Use the time you have wisely. Break up your practice however you want, but try to accomplish as much as you can. You can make the first part all about defense, and you can have the infielders working together. While they are doing that, the outfielders are getting fly balls, and the catchers are blocking and working on their footwork and maybe even throwing. Then the second part of practice can be about offense. Break your team into hitting groups. While one group is hitting, another is running the bases, reacting to each ball that is hit. If you have three groups, the third one could be playing defense, taking balls off the bat. That is why it is sometimes wise to break up the hitting groups according to position. That way, the outfielders could still work on balls off the bat while one group is hitting and another running the bases. You can tailor it however you like.

5. <u>**When taking infield or working with your first baseman, always have him throw to second or home.**</u>

These are the throws he is going to make, so he needs to practice them. I see so many teams in high school take infield. They have the first basemen, playing back. They hit him a ground ball and have him throw to third. When does he ever have to make that throw? I'll tell you when: never. Another thing I often see is first basemen fielding a ground ball and running and touching the bag. Do we really need to practice that?? Every time your first baseman fields a ground ball, have him throw it to second. Make him and the shortstop establish a throwing lane. Work on this. At the beginning and end of each infield, have the first baseman throw the ball to the plate. The only time a first baseman will throw to third is on a bunt play, so you can roll out balls to him at the end of infield and have him charge and throw to third.

6. <u>**Work on pop ups and pop up communication in practice.**</u>

Another neglected practice area. We work on it every day. It helps them with actually catching pop ups, but it also helps them communicate and teaches them their responsibilities on certain balls. Pitchers and catchers should be the kings of communication. When the shortstop calls for a ball, the pitcher yells his name so that everyone else backs off. The catchers let the corner infielders aware of such things as the fence and dugout. Make sure to hit balls that are between the infielders and outfielders. Most of the time, an outfielder can call off an infielder. One exception: an outfielder should never call off a "camped" infielder. In other words, if the infielder has it under control, let him have it.

7. <u>**At practice, make one thing a priority, but practice many things.**</u>

Similar to No. 4, but with a slight twist. If your team is struggling with one facet of the game, you can devote a large chunk of practice time to that. If you like to bunt and your guys are having a difficult time executing, then instead of using the time you have set aside for hitting, use it for bunting. It won't kill you not to have batting practice for one day. It will also make them concentrate. Another way to make them concentrate is to incorporate the bunting within the structure of batting practice, and then take away swings for every time they fail to get the bunt down. Hitters hate to have swings taken away, so again, this will make them concentrate. You can also have a defensive practice, concentrating on nothing but defense, or a day where you do nothing but hit. These types of practices allow you to address any weaknesses that your team may have.

8. **Break the game into small pieces when practicing.**

Baseball is a game that can easily be broken into small pieces. You can involve only the middle infielders, making them work on their double play feeds. The shortstop and second baseman, with no one else involved. They don't have to throw the ball to first. They are just working on exchanges and getting familiar with each other. Maybe you are working with the first basemen, and all they are doing is fielding the ball and throwing it to second. Maybe you are working with the third basemen and all they are doing is throwing the ball to second. Break it up anyway you like. As stated before, it is all about "reps." This can happen before, during or after practice. If possible, maybe the middle infielders come out 15 minutes prior to practice and work on double play feeds. You will be amazed at how much they can improve.

9. **Always make sure to have a team time.**

While it good to break the game into small pieces like the previous point, I believe it is also essential to have a team time. This usually takes place at the end of practice. It can be things like a pre-game infield to end practice or some "team defense" to end practice. This allows the team to get together and work as a unit. Team chemistry and team bonding usually take place at this time. It is very important.

10. **Play the "coach's game."**

This is something I began doing when I first became a head coach. Get the L-screen out and you pitch to your players. They have to hit you just like they do in batting practice, but now they have to run the bases and try to score. A team is on defense and is trying to get them out, just like it was a real game. Your infielders and outfielders will get a ton of work because each hitter is going to make contact. My rule is that if you hit it back at the screen it is a foul ball, but you can have any rule that you want. If you don't have enough players to make two full teams, you can have "mini" teams hit in groups of three or four, and keep track of the runs they score. You can also allow players who might not ordinarily hit take a few swings. Have fun with it. The losing team has to pick up equipment or something of that nature.

Chapter Two

Offense

11. The on deck hitter has an important function.

I see this neglected quite a bit, even in the big leagues. The on deck hitter has the responsibility of being a kind of traffic cop for runners as they approach home plate. He needs to be in their line of vision as they approach, and let them know if they should stand up as they cross the plate, or whether they should slide. I have seen so many runners needlessly tagged because they did not slide, with the on deck hitter just being a spectator. **Remember, at all bases other than first, when in doubt, slide.**

12. If you are going to make your son a switch hitter, do it early.

I have seen so many failed attempts at this when players are in their teens, it just makes sense to do it early so it becomes second nature to the player. Young guys can practice with a tee and a net and get thousands of reps. Remember, lots of reps are essential here. Be patient in games, as success will not happen overnight, but the advantages that await are well worth it.

13. The batting tee is not just for kids.

I played with and against Pete Rose, the man who has more hits than anyone in baseball history. He was a big proponent of tee work. You now see it all around the big leagues and the college game. Hitting off the tee can be a drill that you do alone. You can get tons of reps. You can work on your swing. You can use it as a conditioning tool, strengthening your arms and shoulders (you can even swing a weighted bat while working with the tee, which will improve your bat speed). You can use it to work on your weaknesses. For instance: if you have been having trouble hitting the inside pitch, you can stand closer to the tee and work on getting your hands through. If you are struggling with the high pitch, you can set the ball high on the tee and work on getting on top of the ball. It is a great teaching tool. **Every baseball team should have at least one tee.**

14. <u>Your team should play offense according to the score.</u>

Pretty simple concept, I know, but players sometime lose sight of it. If you are down a bunch of runs, you must play a bit more conservatively. You can't be taking the extra base. Rule of thumb: if you are down late in the game, and you are considering going first to third, your rule should be that if you think you are going to have to slide, don't go! I don't think you should relegate yourself to "station to station" depending on how many runs you are down, but you still can't take unnecessary chances. If you are a team that manufactures runs and does not have much power, you have to keep playing your game. If you have a lead, of course, then you can be more aggressive, especially on the bases. It is a good idea to simulate these types of game conditions in practice so your team will know the difference.

15. <u>Once a hitter makes contact, he must find the ball.</u>

We were all taught as kids that once we hit the ball we shouldn't look at it. We should just run as hard as we can. Nothing could be more wrong. After a hitter makes contact he should take two or three strides out of the batter's box and then find the ball. He needs to know where the ball is. Why?? If he hits a ball directly at the shortstop, and the shortstop fields it cleanly and prepares to throw, the hitter needs to run through the bag. If the ball goes cleanly into left field, then he needs to round the base and look for the possibility of going to second. He is not going to be aware of where the ball is if he doesn't "find" it. I have seen so many base runners run through the bag and down the line when the ball is cleanly into the outfield. Any hope of going to second on an outfield bobble is lost. **Find the ball!!**

Chapter Three

Defense

16. When turning a double play, keep your infielder's hands together.

The two "middle guys" must always keep this in mind. By keeping their hands together as they are receiving the ball, it makes the transition to throwing it much easier. Obviously, this is not always possible because you are sometimes going to get a throw that is a bit off the bag, and you are going to have to stretch for it. If it is only a little bit off the bag, the infielder should use his feet and get his body behind the ball. He needs to stay behind the base and "read" the throw from his partner. Where he receives the ball will determine how he turns the double play. I see young infielders all the time who fly across the bag, committing themselves too early, and therefore cannot react to a poor throw. They need to stay under control. And always remind them of this: **There are no Olympic sprinters in your league. Double plays are not lost because you are not quick enough. They are lost because of bad exchanges. Keep the hands together. Stay under control. Learn the underhand toss. All of these will lead to more double plays.**

17. Corner outfielders should not dive for balls toward the line.

Right and left fielders who dive for a ball toward their respective foul lines better catch the ball. They have no one backing them up, and a miss will result in at least a triple. They must be sure they are going to make the play. Diving toward center field is fine because the centerfielder is going to be there. The exception to this is if the result of not making the catch in the last inning means a loss.

18. <u>Centerfield is the easiest outfield position to play.</u>

The centerfielder gets the best view of everything, especially how the ball is coming off the bat. He should be able to get the best jump and take the best routes to the ball because of this. The corner outfielders don't have this luxury and may not recognize balls that are slicing. That is why playing a corner outfield position is more difficult. That being said, **you should still put your best outfielder in center simply because he is going to get the most action.**

19. <u>An outfielder's arm should be your last concern.</u>

Think of it this way: when was the last time one of your outfielders caught a ball and threw a runner out without the benefit of a cutoff man?? Give me the guy who can go get the ball and hit the cutoff over a strong armed guy any day. Now, if he can do both, then you really have something, but too much emphasis is placed on how strong an outfielder's arm is.

20. <u>A player's feet are more important than his arm when preparing to throw.</u>

At any position, a player must get his feet under him to make an accurate throw. If you watch big league infielders, they almost never throw flat-footed or off balance. They gather their body so it is under control, and then they throw. Work on your young player's feet as much as you do his arm.

21. <u>Catching with two hands is not necessary.</u>

I know what this sounds like to players and coaches of my generation, but the fact is, catching with two hands can often hurt your chances of making the play. It hurts your range if you have to stretch for a ball, and, truth be told, it doesn't help on the routine ball anyway. Trust your glove. (You probably paid $200 dollars for it.) I have never seen a player at any level who "saved" a catch by using two hands. It is simply not necessary.

22. Make your pitchers work on defense.

Once a pitcher releases the ball, he becomes an infielder. They need to practice playing defense as much as the infielders and outfielders do. They especially need to work on throwing to the bases. The throw they seem to have the most trouble with is the one to second base. Work on this daily. Get your feet under you. Clear yourself from the mound if possible because you don't want to be throwing off a hill. Hit the infielder in the chest. Outs are sometimes hard to come by, so you don't want to waste any opportunities.

23. The first baseman's most important responsibility is to catch the ball.

Sounds elementary, I know. So many times I have seen my first baseman desperately try to stay on the bag and the throw glances off his glove and into the dugout and now the runner is on second. As basic as it seems, you need to emphasize to them that **catching the ball is their number one priority.**

24. Your team needs to play defense according to the score.

If you have a five run lead in the 7th inning, you would play defense differently than if you were down five. I will give you an example. High school A is leading by 5 going into the last inning. High school B's leadoff hitter hits a double. All the time I hear high school A's shortstop instructing his outfielders with the phrase "single-4," which means he wants them to throw home on a single. This is just bad baseball. He should be telling them that on a single, they should make sure the hitter does not get to second base, thereby putting another run in scoring position. The other team has a lot of hitting to do to catch up. Do not make it easier. Infielders need to approach defense differently as well. If you have the lead in this scenario, I always tell my infielders to think about outs. They need five runs before we get three outs. I put my infielders deeper than double play depth with a man on first. Make sure of one out. Don't rush on balls in the middle trying to get a double play. Don't be obsessed with getting the lead runner. When you have a lead, those things go out the window. Make sure of one!! If you do this, not many teams are going to come back from that big a deficit. **The best way to eliminate big innings is to make sure of one.**

25. <u>There are four basic infield depths.</u>

The discussion of these various depths mainly concern the second baseman and shortstop. Depth one is where you play when there is no one on base. What determines this is the speed of the runner. If you have a very fast runner, you need to be closer to the plate. With slower runners, obviously, you can play a little deeper because you will have more time. Depth two is known as double play depth. This basically is a calculated risk. The middle infielders play closer to the plate to save time, but they also play closer to the bag, again to save time. It is a risk because you are hurting your range, but it is a risk worth taking. Depth four is playing the infield in. This is what we call a desperation defense. We need to cut the run off at the plate. The entire infield is at the edge of the infield grass. If the situation is first and third, remember, at this depth you cannot defense a steal of second. Depth three is a hybrid of two and four. You are between playing double play depth and having the infield up. The advantage of this is that you can now defense a steal of second, and by playing a little farther back you have increased your range. You can use this if the runner at third is a below average runner. In that sense, it can work just like playing the infield up does.

26. <u>When the ball is put in play, every player on the field has a responsibility.</u>

Like basketball, this is baseball's version of "team defense." I will give you one example because you can then totally get the idea of what I mean. And it happens on a routine ball to shortstop. Batter hits the ball to shortstop and runs down the first base line. Catcher runs along the line behind him to guard against a bad throw. First baseman prepares to catch the ball. Second baseman runs at the appropriate angle to back up first. The right fielder should also be backing up first. The left fielder should be backing up the shortstop in case there is a play at second because of an overthrow. The centerfielder should survey the situation and see where he is needed, most likely also backing up second. The third baseman must also survey things to see where he is needed. More than likely he will remain around the third base bag, but since home is vacated, if the play truly unravels, he may be needed there. The pitcher also needs to survey things to see where he is needed. Simple ball to short and everyone has a responsibility. Practice this so everyone knows where they need to be.

27. <u>Teach your middle infielders the underhand toss.</u>

This is not kid stuff. Every major league middle infielder knows how to do this. If a shortstop fields a ball close to the bag, but not close enough to touch the bag himself, he will always use the underhand toss. Use a stiff arm and follow your throw. This throw has two main benefits: **it is easier to control and it is easier to see.** You do not want the player receiving the ball to have to fight to catch it. A nice easy toss and he handles it easily and then throws to first. Work with your infielders on determining how far away they can be and still make the underhand toss. This is another way they get comfortable with each other.

Chapter Four

Pitching

28. <u>Do not allow your pitchers to throw to location; they aren't good enough.</u>

Sit the catcher right down the middle. Emphasize keeping the ball down. Pitchers ages 13-18, with rare exceptions, do not have the type of command that lets them throw to specific spots. I do this drill all the time to prove my point: during a bullpen session, sit the catcher right down the middle and tell your pitcher to throw 10 fastballs right down the middle. Guess how many will go right down the middle? Maybe two or three. Many of the others may be strikes, but just off the plate. They may have good enough command to throw seven or eight strikes, but they cannot locate like a big leaguer can. Once they reach two strikes, I have no problem with then throwing to location. Doing it before that only causes them to "nibble" and get behind in the count.

29. <u>Strike one is the best pitch in baseball; the 1-1 pitch is the most important.</u>

All sorts of studies and surveys will tell you that if you get ahead of the hitter with a first pitch strike, you are more likely to get him out than if you throw ball one. That is why I emphasize to my pitchers to throw first pitch strikes. Most hitters are going to take the pitch anyway, so we might just as well jump ahead. I preach that they should attempt to throw a "quality first strike," and not one in what I call the "nitro" zone. If you make a quality pitch on strike one, most hitters will take it, and if they don't they won't be able to do much with it. All that said, the most important pitch in any at bat is the 1-1 pitch. If you can get to 1-2, you control the at bat. If it goes to 2-1, the hitter controls the at bat. And what does that control mean?? It puts the hitter on the defensive and I am constantly amazed at what hitters will swing at when they are behind in the count.

30. The 0-2 count is a young pitcher's most puzzling situation.

Lots of pitchers can get to 0-2. As coaches, we preach being aggressive and getting ahead. But we don't work enough on what they need to do once they get there. We don't teach them how to put hitters away. I think young pitchers struggle to put hitters away for two main reasons: they haven't been given the weapons to do it; and they are deathly fearful of giving up an 0-2 hit. Let's address the first one. You get to 0-2 and your pitcher is thinking "now what?" Well, I will tell you what. My pitchers have basically four choices if they get to 0-2. In no particular order, they can: 1. make the hitter move his feet with an inside fastball. 2. throw as good an 0-2 breaking ball as they can. 3. throw a fastball low and away for a strike. 4. throw a fastball low and in for a strike. Those are the choices. You will notice that two of the choices are strikes. I do not always get upset if one of my pitchers gives up an 0-2 hit. We work on making quality pitches to avoid that, but sometimes it happens. Many times during the course of a season, I see teams we are playing having trouble with this scenario. Their pitcher gets to 0-2, the catcher sits outside, and they throw a ball well off the plate. The hitter doesn't even offer at it. That is a wasted pitch. They may as well have just asked the umpire to advance the count to 1-2. If you are not going to put a hitter away on 0-2, then your 0-2 pitch better do you some good. Moving his feet reclaims the outside half. Throwing a nasty breaking ball might make him fish for it, but even if it doesn't, you have put him on the defensive. Again, we work on this on a daily basis to help the pitchers learn to put hitters away.

31. There is a difference between an 0-0 breaking ball and an 0-2 breaking ball.

When starting a hitter with a breaking ball, it should not be your best one. Most hitters, if they are first pitch hitters, are looking for a fastball. If they see spin, they are going to take it. You can actually throw a mediocre breaking ball up there and "steal a strike." Now the hitter thinks he has seen your breaking ball, but in reality, he hasn't. Your 0-2 breaker is typically harder and sharper. You don't want to use this "knockout punch" early in the count if you can help it. We work on this all the time. **Your pitchers need to know the difference.**

32. A pitcher should concentrate on his pitches between innings.

I want my pitchers to use the pre-inning warm ups wisely. If they struggled with their breaking ball in the previous inning, this is the perfect time to get the feel back. This is not just for getting loose again. If they struggled out of the stretch, then use that time to work on that. And they should concentrate on the pitches they are going to use in the game. If his change up is his 4th best pitch and he isn't using it, then concentrate on the other three pitches. Same goes for when a reliever comes in. He should work on the pitches he is going to throw and nothing else. It is just common sense.

33. A pitcher's arm angle is what to look for when he is struggling.

I have an old adage: when the arm stays up, the ball stays down; when the arm goes down, the ball goes up. Watch the angle and release point when your pitcher first starts throwing early in the game. If his arm drops and his release point changes, he is most likely getting tired. Memorize him when he begins and it will be easy to tell when he is tiring or simply not concentrating. **The most difficult facet of managing a baseball team is handling the pitching staff.** This makes it a little easier.

34. <u>Teach pitchers the change up long before you teach them a breaking ball.</u>

You ask any good hitter which combination he hates to face the most: fastball-slider; fastball-curve; fastball-splitter; or fastball-change up, and they will tell you fastball-change up every time. Most good hitters love to hit the fastball. A change up looks like a fastball and therefore often fools them. It will also disturb their timing and often not allow them to catch up to your fastball. One of the keys to pitching successfully is changing speeds, and the change up accomplishes that. It is also, I believe, easier on developing arms.

35. <u>Pitchers can eliminate big innings.</u>

Big innings (3 runs or more) do not occur because the opposition gets six hits in a row. That happens so rarely that it is not even worth mentioning. They happen because the pitcher gives up a hit or two and then becomes what we call "strike zone shy." He starts walking people. Then someone makes an error. I guarantee you if you look back at last year's scorebook to the place where you team gave up three or more runs in an inning, there were walks and errors involved. **Things that you can control.** The pitcher has to stay aggressive in that situation, and the defense, as mentioned previously, must make sure of one.

36. <u>You build arm strength and velocity by throwing, not resting.</u>

Probably the best mentor I had during my playing days was Jim Kaat. He pitched for 25 years in the big leagues and was still effective into his 40's. I believe he belongs in the Hall of Fame. He used to say to me all the time: "It'll rust out before it'll wear out." He threw every day. I have taken that to heart. I have had pitchers who, after pitching in a game, would not want to touch a ball until their next start. They wouldn't even want to throw a bullpen. To build up arm strength and increase velocity you need to throw. There are extremes to this. I am not suggesting that after having pitched seven innings on Monday you should long toss on Tuesday. I do believe however, that you should do some light throwing. I think it aids in the recovery process. If you do follow this suggestion, you will find that in most cases, your soreness will go away much faster. And I have had many pitchers increase their velocity, sometimes remarkably, using this system. It should be overseen by a coach, of course, but I have found that it works for my pitchers. We do incorporate non-throwing days as well. You have to experiment and find what works for each individual.

37. <u>Pitchers need to know when to be quick to the plate and when not to.</u>

Big power hitting catcher on first who doesn't even have a stolen base attempt and we are being quick to the plate! We have a 10 run lead in the last inning and the leadoff hitter hits a single, and we are being quick to the plate. Why?? Your pitchers need to know when it is a base stealing situation and when it is not. If the runner on first in a close game is an average runner, we don't want to turn him into a base stealer by being too slow to the plate, but again, we must know the difference. It is the same with a slow runner at second. You do not need to be quick. Mixing up your looks will suffice. Educate your pitchers as to the various situations. If you are being quick to the plate, with few exceptions, you will not have the same velocity or command. **The hitter must always be your top priority.**

38. <u>Pitchers should experiment with different grips.</u>

Back in the day, I had a pretty good slider. I am always being asked how I held it. I tell people that you can blindfold me and put a baseball in my hand any way you like, and I will be able to throw a slider. I experimented and found which grip worked best for me. It took some time. During my final year in the big leagues, I held my slider much differently than I did during my rookie season. Pitchers need to experiment with different grips for all their pitches, including the fastball. The two seam and four seam fastballs everyone knows about, but if you simply adjust the ball in your hand a little bit from one of those grips, you may get movement you've never seen before. Quite a few pitchers in the big leagues have developed their change ups by using this strategy.

39. Bullpen sessions are vital at every level.

Throwing between starts or in the pre-season in the bullpen is essential to a pitcher's development. It is where he works on his weaknesses and hones his strengths. Each of these sessions should be preceded with a plan. You should be trying to accomplish something other than just throwing. I script our bullpens so that my pitchers will concentrate. We work on things like 0-0 breaking balls and 0-2 breaking balls. We work on quality first strikes. We work on "feet moving" fastballs. We work on our change up. Often times the catcher will give signs and the pitcher will "work" a hitter to simulate game conditions. **I truly believe that a pitcher's concentration habits are formed in the bullpen.**

40. Pitchers should start macro and finish micro.

This is a concept I preach to my pitchers all the time. I believe that aggressive pitchers are the most successful, and it begins with throwing strikes. The first pitch of an at bat should not be headed to the corner. You should try to throw it right down the middle, and down in the zone. That is the "macro" part of the equation. I have found so many pitchers who try to hit a corner with the first pitch and they miss and it is 1-0. Now they have to come in with a strike. Get strike one, and in many cases, strike two, before you begin trying to hit the corners, the "micro" part. As I said earlier in this book, your kids are not good enough to throw to location, especially early in the count. Teach them to go right after the hitter.

41. The best way to get a hitter out is to make him uncomfortable.

And how do we do that? We take him out of his comfort zone. One way is to make his feet move. A fastball on the inside half of the plate, about belt high will do the trick. Do not throw at his head. That only will make him mad. If you make him go into the "jack knife" position, he will not be as likely to reach out over the plate for that outside pitch. Remember: **a hitter's biggest fear is not getting hit, it's getting jammed.** If he is afraid of being hit, he won't be very successful anyway. Another way to make him uncomfortable is to change speeds. Hitters like pitchers who throw everything hard. That is why they hate the change up. They are gearing up to hit the fastball and now you throw a pitch that is 10-12 miles per hour slower. This makes them uncomfortable. **Hitters don't like to make adjustments.**

42. Pitchers need to learn to command the fastball before moving on to other pitches.

Command of the fastball is paramount to most pitchers' success. We spend the first four or five pre-season bullpen sessions working on this. Throwing it for strikes. Throwing it to both halves of the plate. I believe that **everything goes off the fastball.** Once you think he has command of that, then mix in some off speed pitches. I don't think you should start with anything off-speed until he has mastered this. I call these sessions "Fastball Command Academy," a term I stole from Jim Kaat. It also helps build arm strength and emphasizes the importance of throwing strikes.

43. Pitch to your strengths, not a hitter's weakness.

If you are a fastball pitcher and the hitter is a fastball pitcher, what are you going to do? You are going to go with your strength and throw fastballs. **Do not allow a hitter to dictate what you are going to do.** You always want to get beaten with your best pitch. If he forces you to throw your second or third best pitch in a key situation, he has dictated the at bat. So, go with your strength, not his weakness. If they are one and the same, then you should have an easy time!

44. <u>**Don't give hitters too much credit.**</u>

Baseball is a game based on failure. Great hitters fail seven out of ten times. That puts the odds squarely with the pitcher. Be aggressive! Go right after them!! I had a pitching coach during my first year of professional baseball who if someone described a hitter as a "good fastball hitter," would scoff and say "there is no such thing as a good fastball hitter. They don't hit the good fastballs." I believe that to this day. They hit the fastballs up in the zone. They don't hit the ones with good velocity and movement down in the zone. Young pitchers give hitters way too much credit and get "strike zone shy" and start nibbling. That is when they get in trouble.

45. <u>**When warming up before a game, have the catcher be the one that moves.**</u>

When a pitcher first starts tossing with the catcher prior to a start, I am always seeing the pitcher move in front of the mound and rubber to shorten the distance, while the catcher remains behind the plate. I have my catchers move up in front of the plate at this time so that the pitcher can remain on the mound and the rubber. Small thing, I know, but it keeps the pitcher in his "work place."

46. <u>**The most advantageous count for a pitcher is 0-2 after having thrown two fastballs.**</u>

In high school baseball, it is a rule that if you throw a first pitch fastball for a strike, you must throw a breaking ball on the next pitch. At least it seems to be a rule. I see this happen at least 90% of the time. **It is a good strategy, oftentimes, to follow a fastball with a fastball.** As stated before, the hitter will often take that first pitch. If it was a fastball, then he might not be able to turn on another fastball. He will foul it off. Now you have him 0-2 and he hasn't even seen your breaking ball. You should be able to put him away. See No. 31 for ways to do this.

47. <u>Teaching the change up is easy.</u>

The change up is a very important pitch to master. Since it imitates the fastball, it can keep hitters off your fastball. We talked earlier about experimenting with grips, and it is never more important than when developing your change up. There are some simple ways to try to develop the change, but first you must get one main point across: you cannot slow your arm down to reduce velocity. Certainly, doing that will reduce velocity, but the hitter will immediately recognize it and make adjustments. So, how do we decrease velocity? One way is to hold the ball deep in your palm. It is like when you were little and the ball was almost too big for your hand, and you had top use all your fingers to control it. You can also hold the ball at the tip of your fingers. You have to have strong hands. This can take some practice. Another way is to hold the ball like you would a regular fastball, with two fingers. Then add the middle finger. It adds one more "finger of resistance." You cannot throw the ball as hard if you add a finger. If it still isn't slow enough, add another finger. All of this has to do with experimenting. As you grip the ball with a "three fingered" grip, look and see where your thumb is. Moving it around in different places on the ball can also affect velocity. Finally, **when first teaching someone the change up, keep the catchers away.** Just play catch. Don't worry about location. And to help you keep the same arm speed as you have with a fastball, **play long toss with a change up grip.** If you have to throw the ball 100 feet to your partner, you cannot slow your arm down to do it. It works, believe me.

48. <u>The no-fail way to teach pitchers to throw strikes.</u>

We all have had pitchers who simply struggle with throwing the ball across the plate. I have found a way to help them. Once they are loose, have the catcher sit three feet on one side of the plate. Your pitcher takes his normal stance on the rubber and throws 3-5 pitches to the catcher. Then move the catcher three feet to the other side and do it again. Repeat this a few times and then sit the catcher right down the middle. You will be amazed. The pitcher has now zeroed in the strike zone. He was positively reinforced that he can throw the ball where he wants prior to the catcher being down the middle. He did the simple things like "stepping to target" when he had to hit the catcher three feet outside. Now he believes. I have used this with pitchers of all ages, and even have come back to it in the middle of the season. It works.

49. <u>Talking mechanics with your pitchers is not always the way to go.</u>

I often talk mechanics with my pitchers, but not nearly as much as you may think. I sometimes just give them a goal. One of my favorites is a fairly simple one. If one of my guys is having trouble keeping the ball down, I challenge him to throw the next five pitches "below the catcher's mask." It is a pretty easy challenge and most of the time he is able to do it. What it does, without crowding his mind with thoughts of mechanics, is to let his body take over. He will reach out and get the ball there. After he masters that, I sometimes challenge him to throw five pitches "between the catcher's mitt and the ground." This really makes him reach out. I am telling him all the time that the problem is not his mechanics, but rather his concentration. And I truly believe that. **We fill our pitchers' heads with "get the arm over that front knee, and stride less on the breaking ball," that truth be told, most of their mechanics are good enough to throw strikes. Their concentration is not.**

Chapter Five

Base Running

50. Hustle is great, but don't find yourself between the bases while the ball is being caught in the infield.

You want your guys to bust their butts out of the batter's box on an infield pop up just like they would for a ball in the gap. You do not, however, want them to be halfway between first and second as the ball is being caught. If the infielder drops it, then the runner becomes an easy out. **Hustle is good; intelligent hustle is better.**

51. Practice hitting the front of the first base bag.

The shortest distance between two points is a straight line. Teach your runners to run straight for the bag (if you watch, you will be amazed at how many don't) and just as importantly, practice hitting the front of the base. It is the quickest way. Hit the middle or the back of the base and you are wasting time. Miss it all together (which many do) and you may as well have not run down there at all. As soon as you find the ball and you know it has been fielded cleanly, concentrate on the front of the bag and you will have a better chance of hitting it.

52. When leading off first, never look back at the bag.

It isn't going to move. It has been in the same place for hundreds of years, and if you look back at it just as the pitcher is throwing to first, you might get picked off.

53. <u>Never slide into first.</u>

It's dangerous and **it is not quicker.** First is the only base you can run through. If sliding was quicker than running through it, you would see track sprinters sliding at the finish line. Sliding into first **looks like a great hustle play, but in reality, you are hurting your chances of being safe, and increasing your chances of getting hurt.** The only exception to this is if you "read" a bad throw and slide to avoid the tag of a first baseman that has been pulled off the bag.

54. <u>Sliding head first is faster, but more dangerous.</u>

The heading pretty much says it all. You are laying it all on the line when sliding headfirst, and you are more under control when sliding feet first. A couple of points: when running the bases, hold a batting glove in your throwing hand, and never slide head first into home. Holding the batting glove keeps you from getting the fingers on your throwing hand banged up, and sliding head first into home is a bad idea. The catcher wears a lot of equipment!

55. <u>Three phrases for the third base coach.</u>

If your team is going to be adept at base running, the third base coach is very important. When a runner is leading off second, I use three phrases to help him. If I say "OK," that means no one is near him and he can take another step. If I say "careful," the middle infielders are getting close and he needs to stay put. If I say "back," he needs to get back to the base. Pretty simple. Another factor that helps with your team's base running is knowing when you have to look at the third base coach and when you do not. This is mostly applicable when going from first to third. If the ball is "in front" of the runner he does not have to rely on the third base coach. A ball that is in front of him is one that he can easily see in left field or left-center. He needs the coach when the ball is "behind" him in right field and he cannot see it. Practice this by running the bases every day.

56. <u>Leading off first base.</u>

I touched on this a bit previously, but there are a few other points I want to make. You should take your lead to the back of the bag, which simply makes it a longer reach for the first baseman to tag you. When leading, be slightly open with your lead (right) foot. This allows you to open up quicker and be on your way.

57. <u>Leading off second base.</u>

There are two ways of doing this and it depends on how many outs there are. No outs or one out, your lead should be in direct line with the third base bag. With two outs, you should be three or four steps toward the outfield. This is for a couple of reasons. With two outs, it is unlikely you are going to be stealing third, and secondly, it gives you a better angle to round third in the event of a base hit. **Another important thing the runner at second should do is to check to see where the outfielders are playing.** That way, with less than two outs, he can be on his way on a ball he knows is not going to be caught based on the positioning of the outfielders.

58. <u>Leading off third base.</u>

This is the area of base running that is pet peeve of mine. I see runners who lead off while the pitcher is in the wind up. They sprint down the line, and as the pitch is being delivered, they are retreating back to third. They have little chance to score on a wild pitch or passed ball. When leading from third, get yourself in foul territory, and as the pitch is being caught by the catcher, you should have your weight on your lead (right) foot. That way you can get back, or you can have a better chance scoring on a ball that gets away from the catcher.

59. A tagging runner needs to look for himself.

I don't see this too much anymore, but nonetheless, it is worth mentioning. If you have a coach yell "go" to a runner tagging at third, you are going to lose a couple of steps. Let the runner look for himself. On a deep fly ball on which he is going to score easily, I always remind my runners to not leave early.

60. An infield playing "up" cannot defend a steal of second.

If your opponent is playing the infield up in a first and third situation, they cannot defend the steal of second base. Neither the shortstop nor the second baseman can get to the bag in time. If you can teach your runners this, and it is appropriate, second base is there for the taking.

61. Make the delayed steal part of your arsenal.

It is not very hard to teach the delayed steal. When teaching your runners to get their secondary lead, they stop for a split second, and then take off for second. A secondary lead is that little hop a runner does at first after he is sure the pitcher has delivered the ball to the plate. The shortstop and second baseman both observe this. Since they do not see him running toward second, they assume he is not going anywhere. After a couple of hops, he stops, then heads for second. If he has fooled the middle infielders, they will be late covering the bag. If there is a left handed hitter at the plate, he will shield the catcher, and he may not realize the runner is on the move until it is too late. Another key I have to see before employing the delayed steal is to have both middle infielders fairly far away from the bag. If they are close to the bag because of an infield shift on the hitter, you can fool them and they can still get to the bag.

62. Round first with a vengeance.

You see players in the big leagues hit a routine single up the middle and just saunter down the first base line, barely making it to the bag, more concerned with taking off their batting gloves than seeing if there is a possibility for two. Round first hard and put pressure on the outfielder to make a play! If he sees you rounding it hard, he may look up while the ball gets away from him and you proceed to second. **You always want to put pressure on the defense.**

63. <u>Doubles are not lost between first and second.</u>

They are lost between home and first. You see it all the time. A hitter hits the ball and jogs down to first as he is admiring his work. He then realizes he may have a chance for two, so he speeds up and is thrown out on a very close play at second. **He lost that double because he dogged it to first.** You must come out of the box thinking double, and the previous scenario will never happen.

64. <u>A base stealer should never be thrown out stretching a single into a double.</u>

Seems like a bit of a contradiction to the previous point, I know, but it isn't. A base stealer shouldn't get thrown out at second in that situation because he will likely be on second in a few pitches anyway. Play to your strengths!

Chapter Six

Strategy

65. If you pay attention, you can figure out a pitcher's pattern.

I always pay attention to how the opposing pitcher is working my hitters. How he is starting them off and how he is trying to finish them off. What does he throw when he is ahead in the count and what does he throw when he is behind? Does he always follow a first pitch, fastball strike with a breaking ball? All of these things go into my thought process as I run the game from the third base coaching box. As a result, in 2008, we stole quite a few bases at a very high success rate without much team speed. I was able to find my players good pitches on which to run. Many times they ran on a breaking ball in the dirt. If you and your players really concentrate on the pitcher and what pattern he uses, it can be a huge advantage.

66. You can hide a poor throwing catcher.

We have all gone through years where our catcher is not the best thrower in the world. How do we disguise that fact from the other team? The best way is for your pitchers to be very quick to the plate. This, more than anything, will discourage the other team from running. The old adage that you steal off the pitcher is very true. Another way to disguise it is to have your middle infielders take every throw from the catcher in warm ups in front of the bag. You can also just not have your catcher throw during infield practice prior to the game. No rule says he has to. They may find out sooner or later, but obviously, the later the better.

67. <u>**Guarding the lines does not work.**</u>

Teams do this all the time. They get a one run lead in the late innings and they move their first and third basemen onto the foul lines. This, of course, is to guard against the double. You don't want an extra base hit in this situation because that puts a runner in scoring position where they could possibly tie the game. The only problem is that many, many more balls are hit in the areas that these guys are vacating than ever go down the line. So few balls are actually hit down the line, yet we all move these guys over there. What happens? They hit two singles into those holes and you have a runner in scoring position anyway.

68. <u>**A right hander throwing to first is a waste of time.**</u>

You could go to fifty big league games and never see a right hander pick a runner off first. It just doesn't happen. **You throw to first and about ten things can happen and nine of them are bad.** Yet we keep throwing over. When you throw over, you are giving the runner information that will help him steal. If you really want to prevent him from stealing, learn to be quicker to the plate. Throwing over to first is not as big a deterrent as you think.

69. <u>**3-1 is a great count on which to run.**</u>

The pitcher has to throw a strike or it is ball four. The hitter is going to get a good pitch to hit. Putting the runner in motion is going to get infielders in motion and that is always a good thing for an offense. It is like a very safe hit and run. The runner must look in and see where the ball goes, just like on a hit and run. An aggressive team uses this tactic all the time.

70. <u>**3-2 is a great count on which to run.**</u>

See above. Obviously, with two outs, you have to go, but it is also a great count with no outs or one out for the same reasons mentioned above. **One important note: these are great**

running counts, **which also makes them great counts for the pitcher to throw to first.** Your runners must be aware of this.

71. <u>When figuring out your lineup, don't get too tricky.</u>

As coaches, we all do this. We agonize over who should hit where in the lineup. Should this guy hit 4th or 5th? Do we put this guy 8th or 9th? I have learned over the years not to make it too complicated. Keep a few basic things in mind. The hitters at the top of the lineup, during the course of a game and a season, will get the most at bats. That seems fairly simple. During years when I have had a poor offensive team, I have sometimes hit my best hitter, who would normally hit 3rd in the lineup, in the leadoff spot, just so he would get the most at bats. After the first time through the lineup, the lineup is jumbled anyway. The only instance where I really sweat my lineup is a hitter who bats behind a base stealer. He has to be a guy who does not mind taking pitches to give the runner a chance to steal. He can't be afraid to hit with two strikes. I have always maintained hitting behind a base stealer is the toughest job in baseball.

72. <u>When making the lineup, try not to bunch the "same side" hitters.</u>

Some coaches use the platoon system with their lineup. They will stack as many left handed hitters as they have when facing a right handed starter. I think this is bad idea. As a pitcher, the toughest lineups I ever faced were ones that went R-L-R-L. It made it much harder to get in a rhythm. I was right handed, but if you threw seven lefties at me, I was able to get into a rhythm as to how to get them out. I felt that lineup was much easier to face than one that alternated righties and lefties. Another advantage to the "alternating" lineup is that it prevents the other team from bringing in a "specialist" for more than one hitter.

73. <u>The opposite field outfielder should always be shallower than the pull outfielder.</u>

Most hitters cannot drive the ball the other way with much power. If you have a left handed hitter in the batter's box, make sure your left fielder doesn't play too deep. Same thing with the right fielder when a right handed hitter is at the plate. There are exceptions of course. Some hitters have power to all fields and you must adjust accordingly. Most hitters do not, however, and you must guard against playing too deep, probably the biggest mistake young outfielders make.

74. <u>Even if you have never played a team, you can figure out who their fast runners are.</u>

Obviously, the leadoff man will most likely be able to run. The two-hole hitter will probably be able to run a little as well. After that, you can go by position. The shortstop and the center fielder are usually good runners. The second baseman is a good bet. You can look at body types. Lean guys or guys with strong looking lower halves are usually pretty fast. Finally, watch them run down the line when they have their first at bat. As coaches, we seem to always focus on the ball, but it is a good idea to have one coach or player watch each hitter run down the line. At higher levels of baseball, coaches use stop watches to time each player. This really gives you a good idea of who can run.

75. <u>Good hitters hate to face the fastball-change up combination.</u>

Ask any great hitter and he will tell you that the fastball-change up combination is the one he fears the most. We talked earlier about making hitters uncomfortable and this is a great way to do it. It all stems from the fact that most hitters love to hit the fastball and the change up simulates the fastball making it harder for a hitter to "gear up" to hit it. Since the change up mimics the fastball, there is also no spin or rotation for the hitter to recognize like there is for the curve ball or slider. Teach your pitchers a change up!!

76. <u>You and your entire team should watch the opponent's infield.</u>

Watching the opposing team take infield can give you so much information. The strength of catcher's arm is what everyone focuses on, but there is so much more. Are the outfielders right handed or left handed? This can help you decide if you are going to take an extra base because he has to throw across his body. A right handed throwing outfielder who is playing left field and has to venture into left center to field a ball will have a tough time throwing out a runner at third. Watch for the first baseman's arm. If it is weak and you get picked off first, you will want to continue to second and make him throw you out rather than get caught in a rundown. If you are a runner at third and your teammate gets picked at first and you are going to try and score, go when the weakest armed guy has the ball. The shortstop and second baseman will most likely be the cutoff me. How are their arms? You won't know any of these things if you don't watch their infield.

77. <u>It is a good idea to steal bases.</u>

Think about how many things have to go right for the opponent to throw out your base stealer. 1. The pitcher has to give the catcher a legitimate shot. 2. The catcher has to catch the ball cleanly. 3. He has to hit a moving target. 4. That moving target has to catch the ball in good position and apply a tag. If the throw is off line or tails, it is a stolen base. It puzzles me why more teams do not run. If you are a big league catcher and throw out one in three runners, you will most likely lead the league in that category. That means teams have a 67% success rate against you. Look at the stat sheet of any college team and you will see a very low percentage of runners thrown out. Get your team running and you can intimidate your opponent, which saves outs because you won't have to bunt as much, and therefore help you win more games.

78. <u>The catcher, the pitcher and the coach need to develop a relationship with the umpire.</u>

Very few people out there have been christened with the name "Blue." Take the time and effort to learn each umpire's name, especially the one calling balls and strikes. It makes him feel good when you learn his name. If your players are too young to call an adult by his first name, then they should address him as "sir." All of the above will help your relationship with one of the most important people on the field. Another facet of this relationship about which I always talk has to do with a pitch you think he missed. You know why he called it a ball. He thought it was low, or outside, or whatever. You may totally disagree, but if you ask him something like "was that ball down?" and he says yes and you nod your head like you agree even though you don't, you just made yourself a friend. This holds true for the catcher, the pitcher, or the coach. In the long run, it is always a good idea to have a good relationship with the men in blue.

79. <u>Scripting innings ahead of time.</u>

I often script innings ahead of time. I may tell the leadoff hitter of an inning that if he gets on, we are going to hit and run on the first pitch, during which no sign will be given. This eliminates your players missing signs. I will sometimes go as far as to say that if the leadoff hitter gets on, he is going to steal second, then we will bunt him to third, and then the next hitter will squeeze on the second pitch. You can't do this all the time, but when you can it is a great way to ensure no signs are missed. It can also be a solution if you think the other team has your signs.

80. <u>First to third philosophy.</u>

You have probably figured out by now that I like to be aggressive. It is no different in a first to third opportunity. Unless the ball is just scorched directly at the left fielder, I like my guys to be at least thinking about coming to third. This is where knowing if the outfielder can throw, with which arm he throws , and the how high the outfield grass is all come into play. If the grass is really high it will slow the ball down. The outfielder will not be able to reach it as quickly, and the runner can possibly come to third.

81. Take a "cheat sheet" to the third base coaching box.

I learned this the hard way. I did not use the player I should have in a critical situation and it may have cost us the game. I simply forgot who all was available. That is why I now take a small note card out the coaching box with me. Since I manage the game and coach third, it ensures that I don't make that mistake again. I list all of the "live" pitchers, and all of the extra position players. I even remind myself on that note card points like "use Smith to pinch run," or "use Jones for late inning defense." Big league managers have the luxury of not having to coach third and they have a big lineup card taped somewhere on the dugout wall to make sure they don't forget any possible moves. Since I am not in the dugout when we are hitting, my "cheat sheet" serves the same purpose.

Chapter Seven

Baseball 101

I have learned many things from many people during my life in baseball. I have also figured out some things for myself. The following is a compilation of those things that I call "Baseball 101." Some of them have to do with strategy and some with the unwritten rules of the game. Some are simply observations of a life spent playing and coaching baseball. I hope you enjoy them.

82. If your leadoff hitter of an inning makes an out on the first pitch, the next hitter should take a pitch.

You simply do not want to make two outs on two pitches. This is especially true if your pitcher labored through the previous inning.

83. Watch the opposing catcher carefully. He will often give away pitches.

I see this all the time. The catcher calls for an off speed pitch and then creeps forward slightly. The reason he subconsciously inches closer is because he is all too aware that off speed pitches are much more likely to bounce than fastballs. This catcher will probably stay put after calling a fastball. If you pay attention, you can call every pitch. Obviously, you need to make sure your own catcher does not do this.

84. It is OK to sacrifice bunt if you are up four runs or less.

This is true for any time in the game. The reason: One swing of the bat can tie the score. Same thing goes with stealing bases.

Because of aluminum bats and high scoring games in high school and college, the cushion may rise to five or six runs. It is my belief that prior to finishing five innings of a nine inning game, you have free reign no matter the score. There are exceptions to this of course. If you are up 12-0 in the 4th, you certainly should not be bunting or stealing. When you have a huge lead, you also should not be tagging up on fly balls.

85. <u>You do not bunt for a hit when you have a big lead.</u>

That is considered rubbing it in.

86. <u>A first baseman with a bad body who is not good defensively will be able to hit.</u>

Why else would he be in there?

87. <u>Left handed pitchers don't have to throw as hard as right handers to be effective.</u>

I am not sure why, but it is a fact. Actually, I think the reason is because hitters face many more right handers than they do lefties, and it is just a difficult adjustment. I have had teammates in the past say it has to do with the rotation of the earth or the fact that lefties think with the right side of their brains, but I am not buying that.

88. <u>A mirror can be a great teaching tool.</u>

Short of having a camera, looking in the mirror at your swing or your pitching motion can be invaluable.

89. <u>A long toss program is essential in building arm strength.</u>

As mentioned before, you do not throw harder or build arm strength by resting. Your players should long toss a couple of times a week. Don't abuse their arms, but instead pick the good times when they should do this. In the middle of the week, perhaps, when they won't do much other throwing at practice. Pitchers should long toss as well. My rule of thumb: pitchers should never long toss more than 100 feet. They can simulate their motion while doing this. If they throw farther than 100 feet, it makes it extremely difficult to do this.

90. The catcher and pitcher should sit together between innings.

This is to go over what went right and wrong in the previous inning and to strategize for the upcoming inning. It also helps to strengthen the most important relationship on the baseball field.

91. Catchers need to know how to handle each pitcher.

See above point. Some need a kick in the butt and some need a pat on the shoulder. The catcher needs to know the difference.

92. An infielder should not decoy a base runner unless it is going to do him some good.

You see major league infielders "deking" all the time, especially when the runner on first is going. If the runner who takes off is not looking and the ball is put in play, he will not be able to find the ball. If the ball is a routine fly ball to the outfield, the shortstop and second baseman will act as if the ball is a ground ball to one of them. They will pretend they are going to turn a double play. This is to try and fool the base runner into thinking he has to go hard into second to break up the double play. If the infielders are successful, the outfielder can then throw the ball to first to complete the double play. They will also use this tactic on a ball in the gap. They will act like it is a pop up in the infield and confuse a base runner that was not looking. It is all part of the game. What is not part of the game, however, is making a runner slide on a foul ball. The runner from first takes off and the ball is fouled off by the hitter. The shortstop acts as though he is receiving a throw from the catcher. Do not let your players do this. The runner could get hurt, and it would be for no reason. Decoy only if it is going to do you some good.

93. <u>Catchers should not try to frame pitches that are obvious balls.</u>

I will often see high school catchers who try to bring a pitch that is a foot outside back into the strike zone to fool the umpire. Even the worst of umpires are not fooled by this. All it does is make them mad. You make them mad and you lose your credibility with them on subsequent close pitches because they think you are trying to fool them again.

94. <u>On deck hitters should stay in the on deck circle.</u>

Again, one of my pet peeves. My pitcher is warming up on the mound, preparing for the next inning. The other team has their first hitter very close to the plate, eyeing my guy. Little makes me angrier than this. The on deck circle is there for a reason. I tell my catcher in this instance to cease with warm up pitches until the hitter moves back where he belongs. This is just another example of a kind of code that is followed in higher levels of baseball. It also pertains to the situation when you bring a reliever into the game in the middle of an inning.

95. <u>Never yell "throw strikes" to your pitcher.</u>

You think he is trying to walk people?

96. <u>When your pitcher has a hitter 0-2, do not yell "be smart."</u>

If you must yell, say what you really mean: "Don't give up a hit with this next pitch."

97. <u>When coaching third and there might be a play at the plate, do not yell "cut" to confuse the infielders.</u>

It is a bush move.

98. When in doubt, have your runners slide.

I also learned this the hard way and got one of my best players hurt. He was coming to third and I told him to slide. Our opponents fumbled the relay. I saw this and at the last second instructed him to stay up. He hurt his leg and missed a number of games.

99. Practice base running during pre-game batting practice.

Divide your team into hitting groups of three or four hitters. When a particular group is not hitting, have them run the bases. They can react to each ball that is hit, and this simulates game conditions better than just about anything. Doing this, especially from second base, can teach them when they can advance to third. The batting practice hitter hits a long fly to right, and the runner tags. He hits a line drive to the shortstop, and the runner gets back to the base. We do this before the game and every day in practice.

100. There are two things you need to know on a baseball field.

Where's the ball? How many outs?? If you know these two facts, you will rarely make a mental mistake on the field.

Chapter Eight
Adjusting to Your Team's Talent

Every year, I assess my team and through that assessment, determine what kind of game we need to play to be successful. Some years we might have a fine pitching staff but be lacking in the offensive part of the game. Other years the opposite may be true. A coach must adjust on a yearly basis to the talent he has at his disposal. College it is a little different because you can recruit players who play a certain style to fill your needs. In high school, you must adjust to the players who decide to come out for the team. The following are a few of my ideas on how to assess and adjust.

1. Always remember that if you can throw strikes and play good defense, you will have a chance to win virtually every game you play. As stated earlier in this book, your opponents will rarely, if ever, string together five or six hits in a row in any one inning. They have big innings because they received walks or were allowed on base via an error. You can play good defense and throw strikes every game. That is something you can control. If you do that, you have a chance. Offense comes and goes. You may run into a very good pitcher on a particular day, or you may be hitting line drives at people. It happens. But if you throw strikes and catch the ball, you will remain in the game.

2. Run, run, run. I believe in being very aggressive. I love to steal bases and go first to third. Put pressure on the defense to make plays. Look at how many things have to go right for a runner to be thrown out stealing second: 1. The pitcher has to be quick enough to the plate to give the catcher a chance. 2. The catcher has to catch the ball cleanly. 3. The catcher has

to have a good transfer from glove to hand. 4. The catcher has to hit a moving target as it is covering second base. 5. That moving target has to catch the ball and apply a tag. All of these factors, in essence, are why I believe in running. Be difficult to play. Put pressure on the defense. You do not have to have great team speed to steal bases. Pick the correct pitches. In high school, if the pitcher throws a first pitch strike with a fastball, a breaking ball is coming on the next pitch....guaranteed!! Run!!

3. If you have power in your lineup, try to find the "table setters" to put in front of them. Don't worry so much about average. A leadoff hitter should be concerned with two statistics: on base percentage and runs scored. That is it. Batting average is not nearly as important to the leadoff guy. While I believe in being aggressive, it is not a good idea to have one of your fast guys thrown out trying to steal third with two outs and your power hitter at the plate. Trying to steal second in the same situation is OK, but at second he is already in scoring position. Another thing we do is to occasionally turn hitters loose on a 3-0 count. This doesn't mean just the big guys. You have a leadoff hitter up with two outs and runners on second and third, you may want to turn him loose. Oftentimes a pitcher will give you a gift of a nice grooved fast ball because he is assuming you are taking. Not only could this result in a two-run single, it can also promote aggressiveness.

4. When to bunt is also a subject about which I am asked. If you have a great pitcher going for you, you can play for runs early and you can bunt early. If you tack on a run in the third inning and again in the fourth inning using the bunt, the other team is going to feel like they are even farther behind because of who you have on the mound. If the guy you have going for you tends to give up a lot of runs, you have to adjust. Try to manufacture a big inning. If you are fortunate

enough, to say, have a four run lead in the middle of the game, tacking on a run or two with the bunt is a sound idea.

5. The modern game of baseball is rife with specialists. You have long relievers, middle relievers, set up men and closers. If you can form a good bullpen, you can "shorten" the game. Get five innings out of your starter and then have the rest of the game mapped out. One inning outings for each pitcher in the final two or four innings. Remember, hitters hate to see someone new each time they come to the plate. They get comfortable facing a guy a few times because they can begin to figure him out. His release point, what his breaking ball does, and if his fastball has much movement. You bring in someone different and it eliminates that strategy because now they have to learn about the new guy. That pitcher doesn't even have to great stuff. He need only have the ability to throw strikes. If he does that, he can be successful and give you a scoreless inning. Managing a pitching staff is the hardest thing about coaching, but if you think your opponents are beginning to get to your starter, mixing it up is often a good idea.

6. Stopping the other team's running game can be difficult. A few suggestions: work on your pitchers being quicker to the plate; throw a pitch out or two, which will often make the other manager reluctant to run; identify the runners on the other team and realize the players who will stay put.

7. After assessing your team's talent, determine where your strengths and weaknesses are. Address this in practice. If your team has trouble bunting, employ an entire practice working on it. You can also use just the hitting portion of practice and work on bunting. Young hitters really like to take their cuts during batting practice. If you spend a day just bunting, they realize how important you think that part of the game is. Many times young guys just go through the motions when it comes to bunting and then wonder why they can't get bunts down in the game. Same thing applies to the hit and run. Work on it, and you will get better. We practice that along

with squeezing and base running because I want them to be able to perform in the game.

8. During batting practice, have your players run the bases. If your team needs help running the bases, this is a big help. They can react to where the ball is hit and try to make it around the bases accordingly. We do it every day in practice and our players have to take it seriously.

9. If you have a young team, never assume they know anything. Think about having a weekly "Baseball 101" session with them. We do that occasionally at Yale. Simple things like where you are supposed to bunt the ball when trying to move a runner from first base to second (toward first) or where to bunt the ball when trying to move a runner to third (toward third). I talk about counts and situations where I might hit and run or squeeze. I remind them that good hit and run counts are also good counts for the pitcher to throw over. These are just a few of the examples about which we talk. There are many more, and I think it is a good idea to discuss it with your team.

10. Practice with your team the way you want to play. If you are going to play station to station, then practice that way. Work on being very conservative on the bases. If you are going to put runners in motion all the time, then practice that. This makes your players comfortable with the style they are expected to play.

11. Work on situations with your team. Every basketball coach worth his salt has a portion of practice where he sets up scenarios where his team is up four points with two minutes to play. Or he is down four points with two minutes left. Things like what offense to run, shot selection, and do we press are all addressed. Baseball coaches should do the same thing. If you have a four run lead late in the game, and the other team leads off with a double, your outfielders need to be told that if a single follows, they are throwing the ball to second base, not home. Infielders in the same situation (four

run lead) have to be reminded to "make sure of one." Four run lead, man on, and a slow roller is hit to short. He needs to approach the ball so that he gets one out for sure. He should not be rushing so much that he doesn't get anyone. That is called playing to the score and we practice that as well.

12. Realize what each player on your team does well and what he does not do well, and then coach him accordingly. No matter how much it vexes you, if a player simply cannot bunt, don't ask him to do it in the game. I am as old school as they come. I even expect my cleanup hitter to be a good bunter. I am of the thought that everyone should be able to bunt, but truth be told, it is just not the case. You can continue to make them work on any deficiencies in practice, but don't allow your anger to get in the way of proper game management.

A Modern Baseball Dictionary

(Not your grandfather's baseball dictionary)

AB: coaches talk all the time about their players having a "good AB." It is short for at bat.

Approach: you hear this all the time today; a hitter has a "good approach;" this means he has an idea of what he is doing against a certain pitcher or in a certain situation; a typical example might be a hitter who hits the ball to the opposite field when he is behind in the count; he had a good approach.

Bomb: another name for a home run

BP: short for batting practice

The bump: another name for the pitcher's mound

Cheese: used to describe a pitcher who throws very hard. "he's bringing the cheese today." (also know as "cheddar")

Command: if a pitcher has good command, he can locate his pitches where he wants to.

Deke: short for "decoy", as with a shortstop and second baseman make a baserunner believe that the ball was hit on the ground when in fact it was hit in the air; they do this so the runner thinks he has to go back to the previous base; they have, in fact, deked him.

Dinger: another name for a home run

Gas: much like cheese, gas is a good fastball.

Granny: another name for a grand slam home run.

Hammer: another name for a curve ball, usually a good one.

Knock: another name for a hit; Pete Rose used this term all the time during batting practice; he'd hit a line drive and say "That's a knock."

Late life: this describes a pitcher who has good movement on his fastball as it nears the hitter; this is good because it makes it more difficult for the hitter to hit it squarely.

Mash: this means hit the ball really well, as in "this guy can mash."

Max effort guy: used to describe a pitcher who puts everything he has into his windup and delivery; some pitchers are very smooth and effortless; max effort guys are not.

Oppo: used to describe a hitter who goes to the opposite field, usually for a home run; left handed hitters would go to left field and right handed hitters would go to right field.

Pea: a line drive that is hit very hard; the reference means the ball was hit so hard it resembled a pea in size.

Pen: short for bullpen, where the pitchers hang out; it can also mean a bullpen workout, as in "I threw a pen today."

PFP: stands for pitcher's fielding practice.

Pill: much like pea, is used to describe a hard line drive hit so hard it resembles a pill in size.

Pound the zone: used to describe pitchers who throw a lot of strikes; the zone they are pounding is the strike zone.

Rake: much like mash, means a guy can really hit, as in "that guy can rake."

Release point: something I work on with my pitcher every day; it is the point of their delivery where they release the ball; in my view, it is the most important aspect of pitching mechanics.

Repeating: scouts talk all the time about pitchers who repeat their delivery well; that means they have consistent mechanics and are more likely to throw strikes.

Seed: just like pea and pill, if a hitter hits a seed, he hit it really well, making it look smaller.

Slide ball: another name for a slider.

Slide step: this is what a pitcher does to be quicker to the plate to discourage the stolen base; he does not have a big leg kick, which takes longer; he quickens his motion by simply sliding his front leg to the plate as he delivers.

Smoked: hit he ball hard, as in "he smoked that ball."

Station to station: this term is used to describe a team when they are not doing anything out of the ordinary when running the bases. They are not using the hit and run or stolen base, or anything of that sort. They reach base and just look to move on the next one according to what the next hitter does. Most teams will employ this tactic at one time or another. A team that is behind by more that three or four runs late in the game will play a conservative, station to station philosophy because they cannot take any chances.

Texas Leaguer: used to describe a well placed bloop hit, which lands beyond an infielder and in front of an outfielder.

Whip: a modern statistic which measures how many baserunners a pitcher allows per inning; walks plus hits per inning pitched.

Author Bio

John Stuper has been the Head Baseball Coach at Yale University since the 1993 season. He has won two championships, been to an NCAA Regional, and sent 25 of his players on to professional baseball, including left handed reliever Craig Breslow, who, in 2008, became a vital cog in the bullpen of the Minnesota Twins. Stuper himself was a collegiate All American, and fashioned a three year college pitching record of 36-4. That led to his being drafted by the Pittsburgh Pirates in 1978. Later traded to the St Louis Cardinals, he made his big league debut in June of 1982, when he joined the then first place Cardinals. He remained in the rotation the rest of that season, including starting three games in the post season. His final start that year, in the 6th Game of the 1982 World Series, is the game for which he is most remembered. With St Louis down to the Milwaukee Brewers three games to two, he pitched a complete game 4-hitter as the Cardinals tied the Series with a 13-1 victory. The Cardinals won the Series the next day. His performance was, in later years, described by Sports Illustrated as one of the 10 best pitching performances by a rookie in the history of post season play.

Stuper was traded to the Cincinnati Reds in 1985 and played a year under all time hits leader Pete Rose. When his playing career ended, he returned to the Cardinal organization as a minor league pitching coach prior to beginning his career at Yale. This book is a culmination of a life spent in baseball, and the knowledge that has been gained through experimentation and learning from some of baseball's greatest minds.